Vince Carter

Vince
Carter
The Air Apparent

Bill Harris

KEY PORTER BOOKS

Canadian Cataloguing in Publication Data available on request.

The publisher gratefully acknowledges the support of the Canada Council for the Arts and the Ontario Arts Council for its publishing program.

Canadä

We acknowledge the financial support of the Government of Canada through the Book Publishing Industry Development Program (BPIDP) for our publishing activities.

Key Porter Books gratefully acknowledges the following sources for permission to reproduce photographs:

THE TORONTO SUN:
Craig Robertson pp., 8, 30, 32, 46, 47, 55
Trisha Hickey pp., 12,15
Norm Betts pp., 24, 40
Veronica Henry pp., 25
Mark O'Neill pp., 25
Warren Toda pp., 26, 36, 37, 42, 52, 53
Greg Henkenhof pp., 33
Greig Reekie pp., 38, 39
Michael Peake pp., 41
Stan Behal pp., 44
Ken Kerr pp., 56, 57
Mike Cassese pp., 62

CP PICTURE ARCHIVES:
Frank Gunn pp., 11, 48, 65
Steve Savoia p., 18
Peter A. Harris p., 16
Chuck Burton p., 19
Alan Mothner p., 21
Pablo Martinez Monsivais pp., 43, 61
Mark Lennihan p., 60
Chuck Stoody pp., 27, 22
Steve Russell p., 58
Bill Kosrouin p., 35
Chuck Robinson p., 34
David Lucas p., 49
Kevin Frayer pp., 63, 29
Pat Sullivan p., 60
Ben Margot pp., 68, 69
Eric Risberg pp., 66, 70, 71
Bob Galbraith pp., 67, 72, 73, 74, 75

Key Porter Books Limited
70 The Esplanade
Toronto, Ontario
Canada M5E 1R2

www.keyporter.com

Design: Peter Maher
Editing: Janice Zawerbny and Glen Williams
Photo research: Jillian Goddard

Printed and bound in Canada

00 01 02 03 04 05 6 5 4 3 2 1

Contents

Introduction

According to Toronto Raptors head coach Butch Carter, Vince Carter's ability as a basketball player is only "sixty percent of what he can be". A bold statement? Yes, especially in light of the fact that, having played only the equivalent of one full season in the NBA, Carter has established himself as one of the most exciting and dynamic players in the world.

The 2000 All-Star game in Oakland was Vince Carter's first opportunity to perform on a world stage and he made the most of it. Winning the slamdunk contest in spectacular fashion and conducting himself in his usual professional manner, he won fans in all of the 205 countries that watched the game.

Having earned personal celebrity and accolades, and poised to lead the Raptors into the playoffs for the first time in franchise history, Carter is still faced with many pressing questions. How good can he really be? Will he eventually lead his team to a championship? Whatever the answers, one thing is certain, whatever the future brings, it will all be very, very fun to watch.

BILL HARRIS

More than a dunking machine

Vince Carter closed out the 1990s with a century's worth of style and power.

Most members of the crowd that gathered at Reunion Arena in Dallas on the night of Thursday, December 30, 1999 had seen the second-year Toronto Raptors forward plenty of times on TV. Carter's dunks, after all, had become a nightly highlight-show staple in both Canada and the United States.

But even after a season-and-a-half of jaw-dropping athleticism, this game was special.

Carter seemingly got his required poster-shot out of the way early, converting an alley-oop pass—underhanded, no less—from teammate Doug Christie. Dunk number two was a similar alley-oop effort, with the assist coming this time from Charles Oakley.

Carter's dunk in the face of Dallas Mavericks' 7-foot-6 (228-cm) center Shawn Bradley really got the crowd buzzing. But the masterpiece still was on tap.

Midway through the second quarter, Carter was moving through the key at top speed when he took a pass from his teammate, good friend and cousin-by-marriage, Tracy McGrady.

Carter was all alone. It was just him and the basket. What would he do?

Carter's improvisational prowess reached new heights on this occasion. He exploded to the hoop and in mid-air did a complete 360-degree turn before slamming the ball home with his right hand.

A virtual riot ensued in the stands. Players on both benches threw back their heads in wonder.

A few seconds later, with the building still buzzing, the play was stopped at the other end of the court when a Mavericks player was fouled. This was the first opportunity for the game-night video staff at Reunion Arena to show a replay of Carter's dunk on the big screen above center court.

But the arena staff was wary of showing a replay that, after all, pretty much humiliated the home team. Instead, the big screen showed a replay of the Mavs player getting fouled.

The crowd booed. Loudly.

Vince gets a kiss from his mom after being presented with the 1999 NBA Rookie of the Year trophy.

Clearly this was one of those rare occasions in sports where rooting allegiances did not matter. At that moment, there were no Raptors fans or Mavericks fans—or even basketball fans for that matter. There were only sports fans, bound together by awe.

This was one special athlete.

Of course, Raptors fans had known that for a year-and-a-half, ever since Carter burst onto the professional scene in the abbreviated 1999 NBA-lockout season. He went on to win the league's Rookie-of-the-Year award, making him the second Raptor (Damon Stoudamire was the first, in 1995-96) to be honored in such a fashion.

But perhaps more than anything, it is Carter's reaction to his spectacular tendencies that truly separates him from the crowd.

"When I dunk, I'm not trying to get noticed," said Carter, who would sound utterly silly saying such a thing if one didn't get the impression that he was being completely sincere.

"I'm not saying, 'Everyone look at me.' I'm just trying to play hard and get my team pumped up.

"Yes, the dunks are a big part of the game. They help put people in the seats. But I never take them out of context. I always stay focused on team goals, and if our good defense at the other end just happens to lead to some easy baskets, so be it."

In fact, about the only time you'll catch the accommodating and affable Carter with a look of disgust on his face is when it's pointed out to him that, more and more, casual basketball fans view him as a dunking machine rather than an all-around player who shoots, rebounds and defends with equal fervor.

During a road game in Cleveland in Carter's second season,

Raptors guard Alvin Williams was admonished by a courtside fan after he drove to the hoop for two points, rather than dishing to Carter, who might have finished the fast break with more of an exclamation point.

"We didn't come here to watch you make a lay-up, Alvin," the fan said. "We came here to watch Vince dunk, so PASS THE BALL."

Carter visibly bristled when told of the exchange.

"People think I'm just about the dunks," Carter said, shaking his head. "If only they knew that's not even remotely what I'm about."

So what is Vincent Lamar Carter about?

To understand the young man who has been called the next Michael Jordan, a journey into his past is required

In his short professional career, Carter has quickly become the number one draw in NBA arenas around the league.

In a middle class by himself

Describing the emergence of Vince Carter as a rags-to-riches story would be grossly unfair to all the true rags-to-riches stories out there. But does that make Vince's drive to success any less admirable, or even more remarkable?

There are many different theories as to what kind of upbringing is most conducive to producing top-level athletes.

One school of thought suggests that when you start out poor, with only limited opportunities, it's actually easier to commit yourself fully to a dream, be it sports-related or otherwise. Meanwhile, kids from more affluent backgrounds perhaps never really have to commit themselves fully to anything, given the multitude of choices that are laid before them.

Vincent Lamar Carter was born on January 26, 1977 in Daytona Beach, Florida and immediately entered a middle-class life. His mother and his step-father were upstanding members of the Daytona Beach community and the family still calls that city home.

Vince's mom, Michelle Carter-Robinson, was a teacher and, later in her career, a guidance counselor for problem youngsters. Vince's step-father, Harry Robinson, was the band director at Daytona Beach Mainland High School, which Vince and his younger brother Christopher would later attend.

With their school backgrounds, neither Michelle nor Harry put up with much funny business. Vince's upbringing was a strict one, and he was taught to respect others as well as himself.

"Like any other kid, there were times when I thought my parents were being a little too hard-nosed," said Carter, who remains extremely close to both Michelle and Harry. "Looking back on it, though, my parents were always looking out for me, which really makes me one of the lucky ones."

Befitting his middle-class life, Vince did not pick up a basketball at age three or four and suddenly find himself transfixed. That's the way a lot of sports legends go, but it doesn't apply in this case.

Vince was a well-rounded youngster. Yes, he loved sports, playing football and volleyball in addition to basketball. But he was equally passionate about music.

He was an active participant in his step-father's band, playing saxophone and serving as the drum major. He co-wrote his high school's homecoming song and, upon graduating from high school, was offered a music scholarship from Bethune-Cookman. He even found the time to write some poetry in his youth.

While taking part in such a wide variety of extracurricular activities, Vince maintained a B-average as a student.

"I can't tell you whether Vince was actually passionate about his classes," Michelle Carter-Robinson said. "Maybe it was just that he knew he wouldn't be allowed to play basketball or be in the band if his grades weren't up to par. But whichever it was, Vince was a good student, and I'm as proud of him about that as I am about anything."

As Vince got older, however, it became more and more obvious that he was meant to have a basketball in his hands.

By the time Vince had reached the seventh grade, word was out among the Florida basketball community that something special was taking place in Daytona Beach. That was the first time the Carter-Robinson family can remember the name Michael Jordan coming up in the same sentence as the name Vince Carter.

When Vince made the junior boys team at his high school, practically every kid wanted No. 23 in honor of their hero, Michael Jordan. Vince wanted No. 23, too. But when it looked as if he wasn't going to get it, his mom sidetracked the disappointment by issuing a challenge.

"I told him I thought it would be a lot better if he chose his own number and made that one famous," Michelle Carter-Robinson recalled. "He seemed to take to that idea and wound up choosing No. 15."

By the time Carter's high school career had come to an end, everyone in the college recruiting world knew who No. 15 was.

No fewer than 77 schools expressed an interest in Carter, which forced the family to adopt a rather cut-throat screening process to separate the contenders from the pretenders. The list was whittled down to nine; then to six; and finally, to four: Florida, Florida State, Duke and North Carolina.

Ultimately, the North Carolina Tar Heels won out.

"The thing we liked from a sporting perspective was that basketball was No. 1 at North Carolina," Michelle Carter-Robinson said. "We figured it was the best place for Vince."

The best place? Perhaps. But as it turned out, Vince went through a lot of growing pains at North Carolina and learned some hard lessons that he has not forgotten.

As a Raptor, Vince has been able to maintain close ties with his family. Teammate Tracy McGrady is Carter's cousin by marriage.

Powder blues

In the development of anyone's life, the first year away from home usually is a real eye-opener. Vince Carter was no exception to that rule.

"I probably never would have admitted it at the time," Vince said with a laugh, "but I was kind of full of myself when I left high school.

"I was the big recruit, the star from Florida. It's not that I didn't recognize the importance of team play, and I don't think I ever was consciously putting myself ahead of anyone else. It was more of a subconscious thing.

"Maybe I just thought it was going to be a little bit easier than it was."

Going to North Carolina meant the comparisons to Michael Jordan would intensify. Jordan had spent his college years with the Tar Heels, too, but, as it turned out, neither Jordan nor Carter had their most spectacular days there.

The old joke is that nobody but legendary Tar Heels' coach Dean Smith could have kept Jordan even remotely under wraps. Carter faced the same challenges in Smith's system, which accentuated team play to the extreme.

Vince had a tough freshman year. He wasn't playing as much as he was accustomed to doing. His stats were subpar, at least in his own eyes. And, worst of all, he wondered whether he was improving as a player.

"The whole town of Daytona Beach felt like driving up to Chapel Hill (North Carolina) to corner Dean Smith and ask him just what was going on," Michelle Carter-Robinson said, laughing.

But both Vince and his mom admitted there wasn't much laughing going on at the time.

"It made me tougher, for sure," Vince said. "But, man, it was hard on me. It was kind of the first time I doubted myself. I wasn't sure what I was doing wrong."

Vince really wasn't doing anything wrong. It's just that there is a pecking order on a college basketball team and he had to wait his turn.

In his second year at North Carolina, coach Smith allowed Vince

Carter slices between a pair of defenders from interstate rival NC state.

a little more freedom and he started to feel like a phenomenon again.

"You could tell by the look on his face that he was having fun," Vince's mom said. "The spring was back in his step. We all relaxed a little when we saw that, because we knew he was going to be okay."

The Tar Heels advanced to the NCAA Final Four that year, a feat Vince lists as the top moment of his college career.

Bill Guthridge replaced Dean Smith for Carter's third year at North Carolina, and Vince wound up being a strong candidate for

Left: **Due to limited playing time in Carter's first year at North Carolina, most of his highlights took place on the practice court.**

**Vince does his best to jump
over an opponent on the way to
the hoop.**

the John R. Wooden Award, which is given annually to the top player in U.S. college hoops. Ironically, Vince still wasn't the "big name" on his own team, that unofficial honor going to Antawn Jamison.

The following year, the Tar Heels once again went to the Final Four, but for the second straight year they fell a game short of the national final, losing in the semis.

Now it was decision time for Carter.

Given his family's strong educational background, one might think it would have been an automatic choice for Vince to head back to North Carolina for his senior year. But as a basketball player, Vince felt ready for the NBA.

Again, the strength and unity of Vince's family proved beneficial. His parents researched their son's prospects thoroughly, calling scouts, coaches and basketball experts. Their general thinking was that if Vince was not going to be selected among the top 10 picks in the 1998 NBA draft, then he probably should go back to school for another year, specifically to hone his game.

"We wanted independent opinions, from people who had no vested interest in whether Vince stayed at North Carolina or moved on," Michelle Carter-Robinson said. "It was a lot of hard work, to be honest with you. We had to filter out a lot of biases. But knowing now how things turned out, I'm very proud of the way we approached it."

The final consensus was that Vince was a decent bet to be selected in the top five, let alone the top 10.

Before the decision to turn pro was finalized, however, Vince promised his parents he would not forget about his education. He vowed to work toward his degree during the off-seasons and he subsequently was true to his word after his rookie NBA campaign, attending summer school in Chapel Hill.

"Turning pro really wasn't all that dramatic a decision for Vince," Michelle Carter-Robinson said. "You tend to know when something feels right, and after we had done all the appropriate homework, it really felt right."

Born to be a Raptor

Considering the reasonably healthy state of the franchise now, it's hard to imagine what a sorry sight the Raptors were in the summer of 1998.

The team's first season, 1995-96, was a highly successful one. The expansion club won a respectable 21 games and was led by point guard Damon Stoudamire, the No. 7 pick in the draft the previous summer and ultimately the NBA Rookie of the Year.

The second season, 1996-97, brought 30 wins and the potential for great things in the future. But there were storm clouds gathering above the owners' offices.

After general manager/part-owner Isiah Thomas' bid to become the majority owner of the team ended unsuccessfully, he wound up leaving the club early in the 1997-98 season. Most of the players, Stoudamire chief among them, were loyal to Thomas, leading to a litany of hard feelings, back-stabbing and supposedly broken promises.

Stoudamire, who was to become a free agent following the 1997-98 season, made it clear to Thomas' replacement as general manager, Glen Grunwald, that there was no chance he would remain a Raptor for the long haul. Subsequently, Stoudamire was traded in February 1998, just a day after the Raptors had been sold by Allan Slaight to the Toronto Maple Leafs, who up to that point had been bitter enemies with the Raptors.

The Raptors won only 16 games in their tumultuous third season and the roster was a shambles. With the June draft on the horizon, Grunwald knew he could not afford to make a mistake. He needed both a good player and a marketable one.

Grunwald still speaks glowingly about the first time Carter came to Toronto to work out for team officials.

"He had just worked out in Denver, where he suffered a slight leg injury, and he was headed up to see us right after that," Grunwald recalled. "Then, not only is his plane really late, but his luggage gets lost.

"He (got) to his Toronto hotel so late that they didn't have a room for him anymore, because they thought he wasn't coming. We had to scramble to get him into another hotel in the middle of the night.

Although Isiah Thomas promised to stay with the Raptors for the long haul, he left town at the beginning of the 1997-98 season.

Thomas's replacement, Glen Grunwald, inherited a team facing an uncertain ownership situation and a locker room full of unhappy players. Through a series of trades and draft picks he would eventually mould the Raptors into the playoff contenders they are today. Alan Slaight (right) would eventually sell the Raptors to the owners of the Toronto Maple Leafs.

Left: Damon Stoudamaire, the Raptors' first Rookie of the Year, demanded a trade after his mentor, Isiah Thomas, left the team.

Carter has developed a reputation as a young star who is willing to put in the necessary practice time to elevate his game to the highest level.

"The workout was scheduled for 9 a.m. the next morning, and if ever a young athlete had an excuse to be grumpy or difficult or spouting all kinds of excuses, Vince had one. But he showed up on time, in a great mood, and absolutely blew us away with his workout."

Former Raptors' assistant coach John Shumate, who now works

Teammates at North Carolina,
Carter and Antawn Jamison
swap hats after being traded for
each other at the 1998 NBA
Draft.

for the Phoenix Suns, recently recalled the general mood among
Raptors' staffers after Carter's audition.

"We all looked at each other and said, 'He's going to be an All-
Star in this league,'" Shumate said. "Did we know he was going to
be as good as he became? Well, of course not. Who really ever

knows that? But we knew he was going to be good. There was no question."

The Raptors also were conscious of drafting a player who they deemed to be a solid citizen.

Basketball still was on unsolid ground in Toronto. The Raptors had played their first three seasons in the cavernous SkyDome, which was hardly an ideal hoops facility. Most of the news surrounding the team had been bad: ownership squabbles, petulant players, loss after loss.

With a new arena, the Air Canada Centre, set to open in early 1999, the Raptors needed help not only on the court, but they also needed a young player who could help build some bridges to the fans.

"He impressed us as much as a person as he did as a player, which was important considering the spot the franchise was in," Raptors head coach Butch Carter said.

"At one point during the workout, he missed a couple of shots in a row and we noticed a flaw in his shooting technique. I stopped him, told him about it and, bingo, he nails about 10 shots in a row.

"On top of everything else, he was coachable, too. He was almost too good to be true."

The Raptors had the No. 4 pick in the draft that year, and there was some momentary confusion when they selected Carter's North Carolina teammate, Antawn Jamison. All indications before the draft had suggested that Carter was the Raptors' man.

That was, in fact, the case. A trade had been pre-arranged, because the Raptors knew the Golden State Warriors, picking fifth, coveted Jamison. The Raptors wound up squeezing a little cash out of the Warriors, who were worried the Raptors would take Jamison and ship him elsewhere.

The Toronto-Golden State trade was announced on draft night. Bottom line: Vince Carter was a Raptor.

"I'm ready to step in and help get things turned around in Toronto," Vince said, sporting a spanking new Raptors cap.

There indeed was a lot of turning around to do.

Carter's awesome dunks quickly made him a favorite of fans in Toronto.

Rookie of the Year

The only thing that could stop Vince Carter in his rookie NBA campaign was a bunch of lawyers.

A labor dispute delayed the beginning of Carter's first season dramatically, cutting the schedule to 50 games from its usual 82. There was a chance there might not be a season at all, but ultimately an agreement came and the Raptors opened up at Boston on February 5, 1999.

Raptors' coaches and scouts had been raising eyebrows at each other and speaking in hushed tones throughout training camp whenever Carter's name came up. They were impressed. Really impressed. But until Carter started playing real games in real NBA situations, no one would know for sure if what they were seeing in practice and in intrasquad games could be extrapolated to the real thing.

The Raptors need not have worried. Carter started his first NBA game at small forward, scored his first bucket before the game was five minutes old and wound up with 16 points as the Raptors upset the Celtics 103-92.

The hype surrounding Vince Carter started in earnest on that night. With such a short season on tap, speculation about league awards began early, and Carter was instantly identified as one of the top candidates for Rookie of the Year.

Carter certainly was not the only reason the Raptors showed a dramatic improvement in the 1999 season, but he undoubtedly was the main one. At one point, the Raptors actually won 12 of 14 games (simply unfathomable a year earlier) and the club challenged for a playoff spot.

As the season continued, Carter's reputation grew. People started to realize that the Raptors might have come up with the steal of the draft, which had seen Michael Olowokandi, Mike Bibby, Raef LaFrentz and Antawn Jamison selected before Carter.

Raptors' coach Butch Carter said the reason Vince was a starter from the get-go was his ability to defend, rather than his propensity for the spectacular. Casual fans may have had their eyes opened by the dunks, but the experts were more impressed by Carter's all-around game and his noticeably steep learning curve.

Overleaf: **At 6'-7" Carter is comfortable either playing on the perimeter or posting up opponents in the paint.**

Vince lives up to his nickname "Air Canada".

Chris Mullin and Dale Davis can only watch as Carter soars to the hoop for a spectacular reverse jam.

One of the things that makes Vince so difficult to defend is his offensive creativity and his ability to change his shot in mid-flight.

Vancouver's Cherokee Parks
can't bear to watch as Carter
finishes a two-handed slam.

Right: Juwan Howard takes a
hands-on approach to defence.

Carter has worked extremely hard on his jumpshot and has dramatically extended his range since he entered the league.

Carter wasn't perfect. He clearly needed to work on his jump shot and he was prone to the odd rookie error. But as the Raptors had discovered back during Vince's first workout with the club, he was open to suggestion and willing to work.

"The great thing about Vince is that he allows me to get in his face a little bit," Raptors head coach Butch Carter said. "He's coachable, and not every incredibly talented young player is.

"Vince listens to what I tell him, or to what the veterans on our team tell him. I think a lot of that has to do with his upbringing and the people he has chosen to surround himself with. The team always comes first with Vince. It would be easy for him to get a big head and start to consider himself bigger than the team, but he never has."

The Raptors' playoff drive ultimately fell short as they finished with a 23-27 record. But after the final game of the regular season at the Air Canada Centre, Carter grabbed a microphone and addressed the assembled crowd.

Carter "guaranteed" a playoff berth for the Raptors in the 1999-2000 season. Pretty gutsy stuff for a rookie, but Carter had been used to doing a lot of winning at both the high school and college levels, and he had no intention of accepting losing records in the NBA.

As the only rookie in the league to lead his team in scoring (with an average of 18.3 points per game), Carter won the 1999 Rookie-of-the-Year award in a landslide.

"I can't say I'm surprised," Carter had to admit as the media gathered at the Air Canada Centre for the award ceremony. "But I am overjoyed. This is a great honor. Right now all the stuff about me being a great player is just talk. Great players are great over time, not just in one season, no matter how great that one season might be.

"I don't want to be one of those guys who never lives up to his billing. I'm determined to put our franchise in the playoffs and beyond."

What's more, keeping in mind the Raptors' desire a year earlier to draft a responsible, polite young man to help reconstruct the team image, the franchise was thrilled when Carter was named one of four finalists for the league's sportsmanship award.

"I'm one of those people who believes you can be a sportsman while being intense at the same time," Carter said.

"Being a sportsman doesn't mean you're someone who can be pushed around. I think too often in sports we get those two things confused."

Coach Butch Carter has been a major influence in Vince Carter's and the Raptors' development.

At the end of the 1999 season, Vince took the microphone and promised Raptors fans that the team would make the playoffs this year.

Half-man, half-amazing

Vince Carter continues to get better, not only as a marketing entity, but as a player.

That simple fact, which sends chills down the collective spine of every team in the NBA, save the Raptors, has to be separated from the Carter hype to be appreciated fully.

The almost daily accolades are nice. But practically on a game-by-game basis, Carter is experimenting, learning and incorporating that knowledge into his increasingly complete repertoire.

"Even if he isn't even remotely open, Vince could just jack up a shot every time he felt like it," Butch Carter said. "If he did that, I really couldn't stop him. But Vince just isn't that way.

"It sounds kind of corny, but Vince really is a team guy in an era when there aren't all that many of them. He's a throwback."

There has been no indication that Vince is even subconsciously inclined to rest on his laurels. He worked on his jump shot during the entire summer of 1999 and has become increasingly deadly with it, much to the chagrin of defenders who might tend to guard against his killer drives by allowing him a little too much space.

Indiana Pacers head coach and legendary player Larry Bird once said that if Carter could hit the outside jumper with consistency, he would be "unstoppable."

Well, no one ever is completely unstoppable, but Vince seems determined to get as close to that unattainable goal as he can.

Toward than end, Butch Carter challenged Vince to become more ambidextrous.

"Here I had the NBA Rookie of the Year and he couldn't use his left hand," coach Carter recalled. "It was something that had to change. I challenged Vince about it."

There was a telling moment early in Vince's second season when the Raptors were playing Miami.

Carter took the ball at the elbow, shifted it to his left hand, dribbled into the lane, went up strong against a couple of Heat behemoths, got fouled and still managed to lay the ball in...with his left hand, of course.

Coach and player caught each other's eyes and exchanged knowing smiles.

Carter has developed a fade-away jumper that is almost impossible to defend.

"Man, Butch rode me hard," Vince said. "When that ball went in, I wanted to call a timeout, walk over and smack him in the head.

"I have a lot of people around me who never would allow (complacency) to happen starting with my coach and the other players on my team, right down to my mom."

The comparisons to Jordan are going to continue, despite the obvious personality differences between the two. Jordan attacked the game with fury, viewing every possession as a personal test; Carter continues to be a genuinely nice guy who just happens to be a great basketball player.

Typically, Carter is honored by the comparisons to Jordan, but he is adamant about carving his own niche.

"I've never even spoken to him about it," Carter said, the "him" being you-know-who. "I try to stay away from it and that wouldn't help the situation. No disrespect intended, but it's a comparison that can't possibly benefit me in the long run.

"I don't have the anger that (Jordan) had. I come from a different background. I like to have fun when I'm playing. The game is enjoyable to me. I'm not saying I'm not passionate, because I am. But I think I show it in different ways."

As Vince's spectacular feats pile up, does his coach ever grasp the opportunity during a game to take a step back, observe Vince's overall impact and say to himself, "thank God he's on my side"?

"Not during games," Butch Carter said. "But when I say my prayers at night, I'm glad Vince is on my team."

Raptors' teammate Charles Oakley once described Vince Carter as "half-human, half-man." No one is quite sure to this day exactly what Oakley meant, but it undoubtedly was a compliment.

Los Angeles Lakers behemoth center Shaquille O'Neal later put a more understandable spin on Oakley's suggestion, referring to Vince Carter as "half-man, half-amazing."

If either Oakley or O'Neal is even half right, Raptors' fans are in for a treat for as long as Vince Carter wears a Toronto uniform.

Bruising forward Charles Oakley provides the young Raptors with the physical presence and veteran leadership necessary to become playoff contenders.

Vince Carter is constantly compared to fellow North Carolina alumnus and basketball legend, Michael Jordan. He tries to downplay these comparisons but with each new accomplishment, more pressure is placed on him to fill the void left by the superstar's retirement.

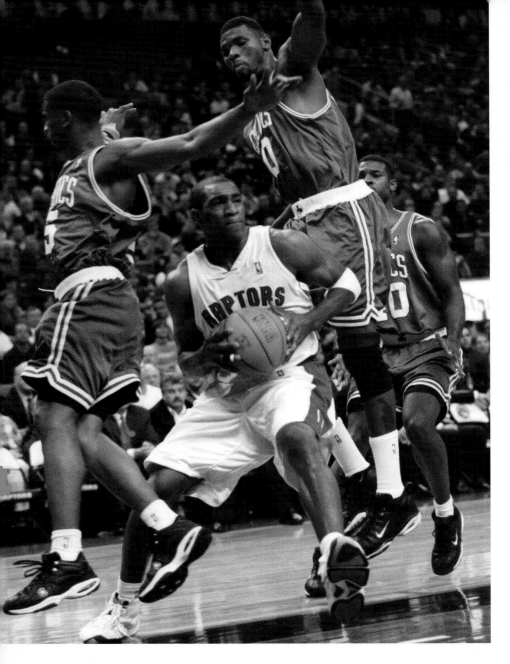

Left: Following the success of his rookie season, this year Carter is often double and triple teamed by the opposition.

Right: By extending his shooting range Vince has forced defenders to remain close to him, making themselves vulnerable to his explosive drives to the hoop.

Overleaf: Carter's explosive leaping ability allows him to hang in the air and put up soft shots around the rim while his power lets him go through or, when necessary, directly *over* defenders caught between him and the rim.

Sophomore Year

The early month's of the year 2000 were some of the best in Vince Carter's life but they were not without their difficult moments.

He kept saying that being passed over for the 2000 U.S. Olympic team didn't really bother him. It wasn't important, he said. A side issue. A non-issue, even.

That was the politician in him talking. But nobody believed his words. His eyes and his borderline grumpy mood told a different story.

Carter went into what for him could be described as a mini-slump in the wake of the Olympic news. It's not that he was sulking, but a smidgen of the joy in his game seemed to have dissolved.

Then came the night of Friday, January 14, 2000, at the Air Canada Centre.

The Raptors' opponent that night was the Milwaukee Bucks, who happened to feature guard Ray Allen. Ostensibly, it was Allen who had been selected for the Dream Team instead of Carter.

Knowledgeable basketball fans knew full well that Allen was a worthy choice. But his selection had led to a swell of controversy, to the point where he was starting to feel defensive about what should have been one of the highlights of his professional career.

The atmosphere at the Air Canada Centre that night reeked of a showdown. Neither Carter nor Allen had instigated this gunfight, but neither of them was going to back down, either.

Vince's effort was nothing less than Olympian. He merely put on the most spectacular show of his pro career.

Carter scored 47 points—establishing both a new career-high and a new franchise record—as the Raptors beat the Bucks 115-110 before a frenzied throng of 19,246.

Did Carter think about getting to 50?

"I did, I did," Carter said. "I told Muggsy (Bogues, Raptors guard) that I needed three free throws, but unfortunately he didn' t pass me the ball (in the final minute of the game)."

Of course, Carter was kidding. But there was no fooling around when he was asked if he had just played his best career game.

"Oh yeah, no doubt," he said. "But the reason I say that is not

When Vince was passed over by the selection committee for the US Olympic team and Milwaukee Bucks guard Ray Allen was chosen in his place, it added fuel to an already heated rivalry between the Raptors and the Bucks. In their first meeting after the Olympic team was announced, Carter scorched Milwaukee with a season high 47 points.

the scoring. I was able to pass, rebound and defend a little also. That's what makes it special."

Raptors head coach Butch Carter, as usual, tried to hose down the hyping of his young star.

"He showed he can make a statement ... for one game," the coach said. "It's a heavy burden for a (player as young as Carter) to have to score that many points for us to win.

"But how do you guard him if he's making jumpers?"

With great difficulty.

Vince, naturally, rejected the notion that he had been intent on sending any sort of personal message to Allen. But when Butch Carter was asked what had prompted Vince to explode offensively, the coach said, "I think it's that he's not walking into an Olympic Stadium."

Vince demonstrated how he responded to disappointment, but how would he respond to the inflated expectations of millions of fans expecting to see the show of their lives at the All-Star Game.

Vince Carter's 1999-2000 totals in All-Star voting by fans placed him second.

All-time, that is.

According to the league, Carter's final vote total of 1,911,973 was the second-highest in history. Chicago's Michael Jordan amassed 2,451,136 votes in 1997.

Carter thus became the first player in Raptors history to be an All-Star and he was slated to start at forward for the Eastern Conference in the 49th NBA classic, to be held in Oakland.

"It is great, not just for me, but for the city of Toronto," Carter said. "It helps put us on the map.

"Maybe now we'll get some TV time."

Raptors' coach Butch Carter agreed that Vince's fan-voting landslide had far-reaching implications for the future of Toronto basketball.

"It is huge for the franchise," the coach said. "It is good to know there is a basketball god."

Amazingly, Vince was named on about half of the 3.9 million ballots cast. He took the lead in voting in late December and never relinquished it.

"It makes you wonder just how many fans you have," Carter said.

Of course, all those fans, all that adulation and all the attention can cause some problems, too.

"He's still only a human being," said Vince's mom, Michelle Carter-Robinson. "He still has to deal with all the other things

Carter celebrates a Raptors victory at center court of the ACC.

people have to deal with in their lives. And you know what? Life can be very difficult sometimes."

Vince Carter has stood out from the crowd since he was a little kid, thanks to his immense athletic skills. But since becoming a NBA player, his star has risen so fast, some of the adjustments he has been forced to make have been painful ones.

"Recently I was in Toronto and we had a rare afternoon with no commitments," Vince's mom said. "I said to Vince, 'Why don't we go to the mall and do some shopping, just to relax.'

"Vince didn't say a thing. He just had a blank look. And then he

Overleaf: **Two of the NBA's brightest young stars, Vince Carter and Kobe Bryant, share a laugh during a break in the action, but things get serious during play as Kobe applies a stiff-arm to Vince's forehead. They faced off against each other at the 2000 All-Star game in Oakland with Bryant representing the Western Conference and Carter the Eastern.**

finally said, 'Mom, I can't go to the mall ... remember?'

"For a moment, I'd forgotten. He lives, we live, in a fishbowl. I don't think we had any idea it would get this big this fast. We're treading new ground. Every day something unexpected comes up."

Off the court, managing Vince Carter's image and business interests requires a full-time staff of 18 people. During the season, each day, Team Vince gets three to four large boxes of news clippings about Carter from around the world. Staff categorizes what has been said, and then those clips are distributed to 20-30 marketing people and sponsors on a weekly basis.

About 10,000 pieces of mail are received every three or four weeks. And that's not even counting e-mail. There is a Vince Carter clothing line. There is a Vince Carter charitable foundation. There are commercial spots, plus offers to do TV sitcoms and movies.

But Vince is well aware that everything stems from his game. If he doesn't play well, the empire fizzles.

"It is not easy to be him," coach Carter said. "He's learning that right now.

"But the truth is, as his coach, I don't care how much pressure he's feeling, he has a job to do. Those are the boots he has to wear. He doesn't accept an excuse from me, nor should he, at the end of a game when I have to draw up a play for us to try to win.

"I say, 'Hey, you've got a brain. No excuses. You have to make the right play for the team.'"

If that sounds like a lot of pressure, well, it is. But that's what being the best is all about.

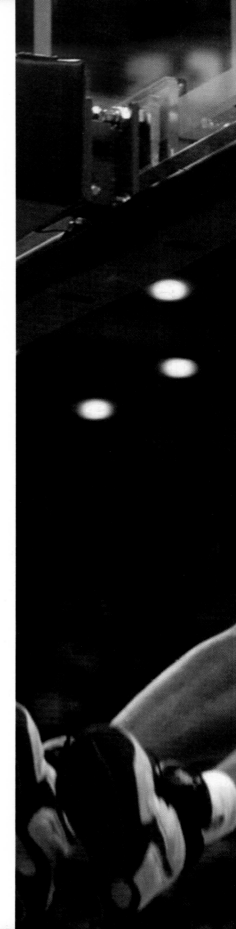

Sometimes Vince surprises even himself: He celebrates after a comeback victory over Grant Hill and the Detroit Pistons at the ACC.

Carter demonstrates to fans in Houston that he doesn't actually need to look at the rim in order to dunk on the Rockets.

Overleaf: Although the Raptors have progress has outpaced the Grizzlies since the two Canadian teams entered the league, Vancouver managed to defeat the Raptors when they visited Toronto January 9, 2000.

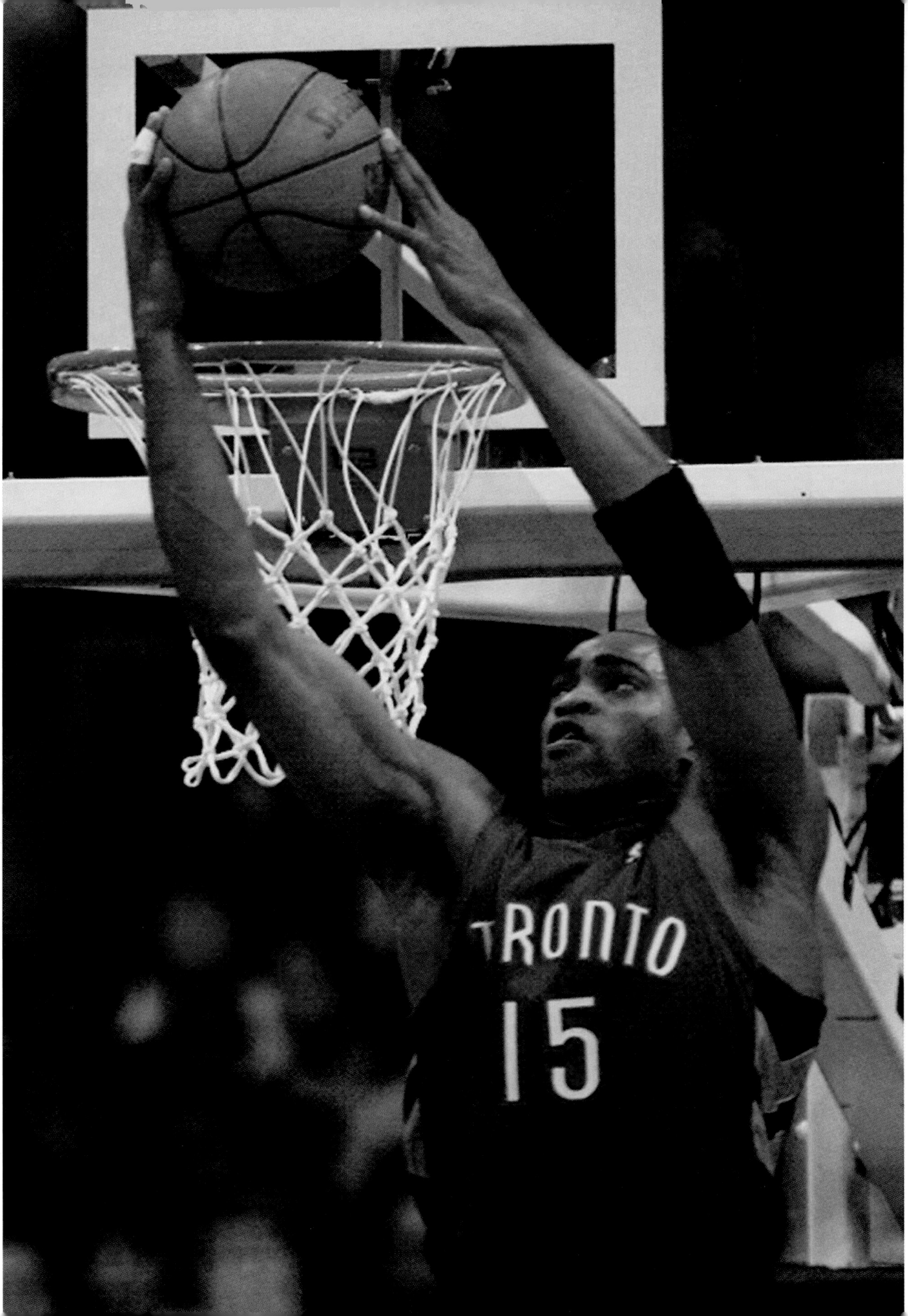
15

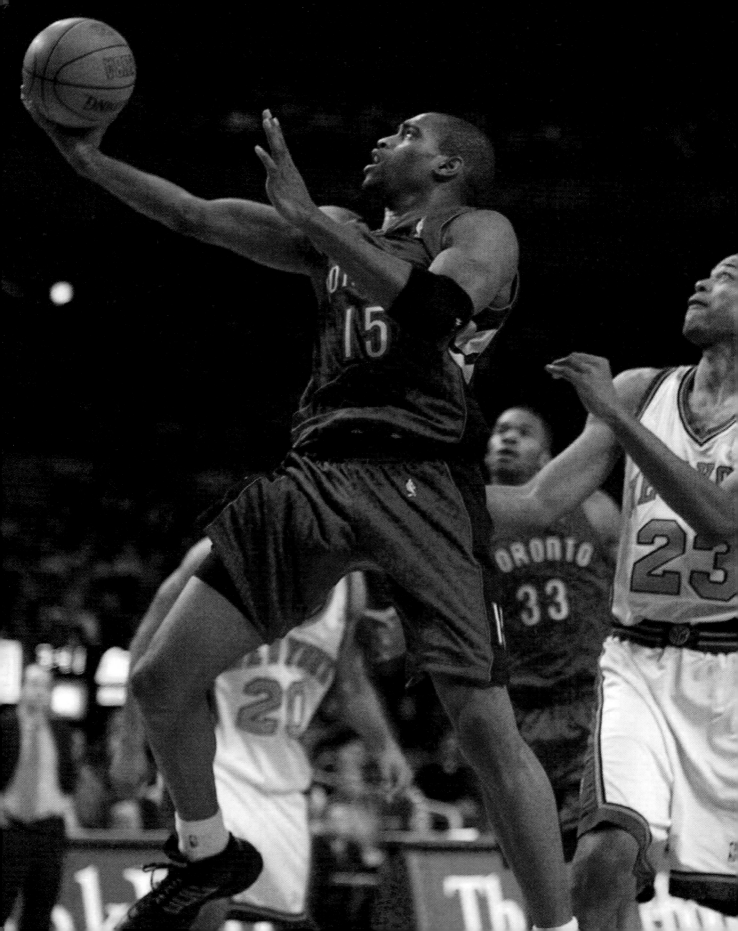

Previous page:
No Chance: A pair of Cleveland Cavaliers can't even come close to the ball as Carter lofts a baby-hook over their heads.

Right: As his profile has increased so has the defensive attention Carter receives from opposing teams.

Left: Vince drives hard to the basket at Madison Square Garden in New York as former Raptor Marcus Camby looks on helplessly.

All-Star 2000

At the 2000 All-Star Game in Oakland, California, amid all the superstars of the NBA, there was one thing that every fan wanted to see—Vince Carter in the Slam Dunk Contest. They didn't go home disappointed.

Carter served notice that he was in a league of his own with his first attempt of the competition. After a surprising display of showmanship, Vince stepped up and executed an incredible 360, punctuated by a rim shaking windmill slam. Fellow All-Stars at courtside were awestruck. Olympic nemesis Ray Allen was literally floored, as he fell flat on his back in amazement.

He didn't stop there. Carter displayed a stunning array of talents with dunks that included catching a pass mid-air, passing it between his legs into a right-handed tomahawk and finishing one of his dunks with his arm stuck in the hoop up to his elbow. Vince was the runaway winner of the contest and prompted slam-dunk legend "Dr. J", Julius Erving to declare that "Vince Carter is the best dunker on the planet".

The All-Star game itself was almost anti-climactic after his dunk contest victory, but Carter performed well and looked right at home on the same court as the best players in the world. He had two spectacular moves in the first quarter and finished with a respectable 12 points but his impact on the weekend was far greater. He stunned fans and players alike and cemented his status as the NBA's next great superstar.